Jokes...

I Have a Million of Them

by

Brownie J. Andrews, Jr.

Chapter 1 - Animal Jokes

Chapter 2 - Food Jokes

Chapter 3 - AirPlane Jokes

Chapter 4 - Hospital & Doctor Jokes

Chapter 5 - Wizard of Oz Jokes

Chapter 6 - Insect & Bug Jokes

Chapter 7 - Nationality Jokes

Chapter 8 - Clown Jokes

Chapter 9 - State Jokes

Chapter 10 - Music Jokes

Chapter 11 - Funny / Corny Jokes

Chapter 12 - School Jokes

Chapter 13 - Police Jokes

Dedication

I would like to dedicate this book of laughter to my father and loving mother which is in heaven.

My wife DanElla of over 35 years who has stuck with me through the good times and the great times and my 3 awesome children Jason, Mykel, Katrina and 2 grandchildren Terrell and Maya (my princess).

Enjoy the book!

What kind of music do they play in a soda factory?

They play 'Pop' music!

Chapter 1 - Animal Jokes

Joke: What is the difference between a hippo and a nurse?

Answer: About 30 pounds and a pair of scrubs.

...

Joke: Where do sheep get their haircut?

Answer: At the baaaa-bershop.

...

Joke: What is a giraffe's favorite fruit?

Answer: A neck-ta-rine.

...

Joke: What do you get when you cross an insect with a rabbit?

Answer: You get bugs-bunny.

...

Joke: What kind of birds hang around churches today?

Answer: Birds of Prey.

Joke: What happened to the frog that was illegally parked?

Answer: He got 'toad'.

...

Joke: What do you call a seagull after it's flown over San Francisco Bay?

Answer: A bagel.

...

Joke: What did the baby colt say when he coughed?

Answer: "Excuse me", (cough cough) "Excuse me. I'm a little horse."

Joke: Why didn't they let the baby cub inside the grocery store?

Answer: Because he had 'bear' feet.

...

Joke: What do you call a cow, after it's given birth to its baby calf?

Answer: You call it de-cafa-nated.

...

Joke: What did the duck say after it ate a delicious meal at I-hop restaurant?

Answer: He said to the waitress just put it on my bill.

...

Why did the chicken run away from the school house?

Answer: Because it had People-pox, not chicken pox but people-pox.

...

Joke: Why did the elephant quit his job at the Barnum and Bailey Circus?

Answer: Because he was getting paid peanuts.

...

Joke: What do you get when you cross a centipede with a parrot?

Answer: You get a walkie-talkie.

Joke: What do you call a seagull after it's flown over San Francisco Bay?

Answer: You call it a Bay-gull.

...

Joke: What do Bumblebee's use when it gets very cold outside in the wintertime?

Answer: They use yellow jackets.

...

Joke: Why do birds fly south for the winter?

Answer: It's too far to walk.

Joke: Why do cows wear bells?

Answer: Because their 'horns' don't work.

...

Joke: Why was it so hard to play cards on Noah's Ark?

Answer: Because he had too many 'cheetahs' on the ark.

...

Joke: Why did the little turtle cross the road?

Answer: To get to the shell station.

Joke: The boy's dad just purchased a brand-new SUV. The next day he decided to take his son for a ride. His son and his little puppy were inside.

And he said, "Son I'm going to make a quick stop", and the boy accidentally let down the window and his little puppy jumped out of the window.

What did the little boy say when the little puppy ran down the street? He said, and with hesitation, "Dog gone!"

...

Joke: What do you get when you cross a tiger with a MRI machine?

Answer: You get a 'CAT' scan.

Joke: What does a farmer use to count his cattle and cows with?

Answer: He uses a 'Cow-culator'.

...

Joke: What do you get when you cross a sheep with and iron pill?

Answer: Steel Wool.

...

Joke: Why do hummingbirds hum?

Answer: Because they don't know how to sing.

Joke: What do bees use to style their hair with?

Answer: They use a honeycomb.

...

Joke: What do you call two snakes on your windshield?

Answer: You call them windshield-vipers.

...

Joke: What do you call a cat after it's licked a half of a pint of lemonade?

Answer: You call it a sour puss.

Joke: What do you call a cat after it's lick a half of a pint of lemonade?

Answer: You call it a sour puss.

...

Joke: What do you call a cat after it has eaten a ball of yarn?

Answer: You don't call it kittens, you call it mittens.

...

Joke: What happens when you get bit by a T Rex?

Answer: You get a 'dina-sore'.

Joke: What kind of key can not open a door?

Answer: A 'Tur-key'.

...

Joke: What do you call 300 bunnies jumping on a bald man's head?

Answer: You call it a receding 'hare-line'.

...

Joke: Why was it so hard for the Easter Bunny to pass out Easter eggs after a rainy day?

Answer: Because he had a very bad 'hare' day.

What's the difference between a dollar bill and a duck?

Answer: One has its face on a bill and the other it's Bill on a face.

...

Joke: When Michael Jordan was playing for the Chicago Bulls. What would you call him when he was sleeping?

Answer: A sleeping 'bull-dozer'

...

Joke: Do you know who really needs a mink?

Answer: A mink.

Joke: A horse named Ed walked into the neighborhood bar. And the bartender asked him why the long face?

...

Joke: Why did the turkey cross the road?

Answer: Because the chicken was on vacation.

...

Joke: What did the mother skunk say to her teenage skunk as he drove away?

Answer: She hollered out, "Don't stink and drive".

Joke: What do you call a cow that has no legs?

Answer: You call it 'ground' beef.

...

Joke: Why do cows like to go to the theater?

Answer: Because they like 'mooo-vies'.

Why did the pickle close its eyes in the refrigerator?

Because the salad was dressing

Chapter 2 - Food Jokes

Joke: Why didn't the sandwich like the pickle?

Answer: Because he thought he was a big 'dill'

...

Joke: Did you hear Buckwheat decided to become a Muslim?

Answer: Now he wants to be called Kareem of wheat.

Joke: How does a Cub Scout, become a Boy Scout?

Answer: He has to eats a brownie.

...

Joke: What kind of a dress can't you eat?

Answer: And ad-dress. Get it? Address.

...

Joke: What is Santa Clause favorite chocolate treat?

Answer: Chocolate Ho-Hoes.

Joke: Why are apples called apples?

Answer: Because they don't come in pairs.

...

Real Story: Just the other day I was out of town. I had to take care of a small banking error and while conversing with the banker, I stated; "when the world throws you lemons", and she shouted back; "Just take 'em".

...

Joke: Why did the pickle close its eyes in the refrigerator?

Answer: Because the salad was dressing

Joke: What is a witch's favorite hot dog?

Answer: Hollow-Weenies

...

Joke: What do snowmen eat for breakfast in the morning?

Answer: They eat frosted flakes.

Joke: Where did Burger King and dairy queen go for their honeymoon?

Answer: They went to White Castle.

Joke: Why did the little boy put hammers on his mother's dinner table at night?

Answer: Because for dessert she was serving 'pound cake'

...

Joke: One day a carrot, onion, pickle and a head of lettuce decided to have a race. Which one won the race?

Answer: The head of lettuce. Why? Because it was 'ahead'

Joke: Once upon a time there were two carrots. A boy carrot and a girl carrot. One lovely bright summer day, they decided to walk to the neighborhood zoo. Unfortunately, the girl carrot was injured by a car.

She was rushed to the emergency room, when the doctor came back. to give his diagnosis he replied, "Mr. Carrot, I have some good news and I have some bad news.

The good news; she's going to live". And he was relieved. "The bad news is she's going to be a vegetable the rest of her life".

Joke: Why did the little boy stare at the orange juice carton so long at the breakfast table?

Answer: Because the orange juice carton said 'concentrate'.

...

Joke: Why did the little boy sprinkle sugar on his dad's head?

Because for breakfast, he wanted sugar pops.

...

Joke: What do you get when you cross Bruce Lee with a pig?

Answer: You get a pork chop.

Joke: What did the little grape say when the elephant stepped on him?

Answer: The poor little grape didn't say anything. He just 'wined'.

...

Joke: What is Popeye's favorite cologne?

Answer: Olive oil

...

Joke: What did Mama corn ask the Daddy corn at the picnic?

Answer: Where's the pop, Corn?

Joke: What did the Baby corn ask his Mama corn at the movie theater?

Answer: Where my PoPcorn.

...

Joke: What do you call a witch on the beach?

Answer: A sand-witch.

...

Joke: What did one deli worker say to the other deli worker when she was very mad at her?

Answer: You're a bunch of baloney.

Joke: Why did the man put his car in the oven?

Answer: Because he wanted a 'Hot-Rod'.

...

Joke: What type of beverage do boxers love to drink?

Answer: They like fruit punch

...

Joke: Why did the girl watermelon tell the boy watermelon they could not get married?

Answer: She replied, "Now you know we Cantaloupe"

Joke: What do you call a dog in Alaska?

Answer: You call him a chili dog.

...

Joke: Did I ever tell you the joke about the little boy named Johnny? That he went to the store and bought a pound of butter? They replied, "No". OK.

Answer: I'll let it slide.

Why was the groom mad on his wedding day?

Because the bride married the Best-Man

Chapter 3 - AirPlane Jokes

Joke: why did the children do their homework on the airplane?

Answer: Because they desire a higher education.

...

Real Life Story:

While flying back home from Chicago.

A baby began to holler and cry very loud.

And I said to my son, "do you know why that little baby is crying?"

He replied, "Yes, the baby is crying because of the pressure in the airplane that is making his ears hurt".

And I said to him, "No, the baby is crying because it's very 'ear-ritated'. Get it? The baby is very irritated. OK.

Why did the oak tree go
to the hospital?

Because he had to visit his cousin
which was in Tree-age.

Chapter 4 - Hospital & Doctor Jokes

Joke: Why did the computer go to the Chiropractor?

Answer: Because he had a Slip-Disc.

...

Joke: Why did the cookie go to see his doctor?

Answer: Because he felt very crummy

Joke: Finally, Mr. Jones decided at the age of 87 years old it was time to stop spreading his oats it's all over the place. He wanted a vasectomy.

So, on the day of the procedure he decided to get dressed up in a very nice beautiful brand new tuxedo. Right before the surgeon started to surgery on him he asked him, "Mr. Jones, why are you wearing a tuxedo to your vasectomy?".

He quickly replied, "Well" …. with no hesitation, he replied, "I might as well look impotent, if I'm going to be impotent"

Joke: Why did the house call the doctor?

Answer: Because he had a window 'pain'

...

Joke: How can you tell a Female chromosome from a Male chromosome?

Answer: By its Jean's

...

Joke: What did the left eye say to the right eye?

Answer: Something in between us, smells

Joke: Once upon a time there were three doctors and they all died.

The first doctor goes up to heaven and he thinks that he is going to bust heaven wide open. But Saint Peter stopped him at the Golden Gate asked him, "What did you do when you are on earth?"

He replied, "Well, I was a medical doctor and I had my own office and I gave medication on time and I had great bedside manners", and he looked at his list and said, "OK stay in heaven as long as you like. You pass".

So, the second doctor walked up and St. Peter asked him, "What did you do when you are on earth?" He said, "Well I was a pediatrician and I had little children and I took care of my babies. I gave them sugarless candies and I gave them Band-Aids with smiley faces". St. Peter looked at his records and said, "Go to heaven stay as long as you like". Yeyy, he was happy.

Finally, the third doctor walked up to the gate and he couldn't look St. Peter in the face. He said, "What did you do when you were on earth? The doctor looked replied a bowed down head saying, "I was a HMO doctor", and Saint Peter replied, "Well, unfortunately, you can only stay in heaven three days and you've got to go".

Joke: Where do ships and boats go when they get very sick?

Answer: They go to the 'dock'

What do Lawyers say, right before they go to bed at night?

They say, "I rest my case"

Chapter 5 - Wizard of Oz Jokes

Joke: How do you make a witch itch?
Answer: Just take away the W and watch that witch, itch all over.

...

True Story: Just last week I had to go out of town to take care of a family emergency and on the way back flying from Portland to Chicago. The lovely couple sitting next to me the wife said; "It's so hot in here on this plane", and she reached for the air conditioner nozzle and as she said that I was playing a game on my phone, The Wizard of Oz, "I quit" Nick replied to her, [in a high pitch voice] "I'm melting ". I'm melting.

Why do spiders like to hang around the computers nowadays?

Because of all the Websites!

Chapter 6 - Insect & Bug Jokes

Joke: Why do spiders like to hang around computers nowadays?

Answer: Because of all the Web sites.

...

Joke: What did the Mother skunk say to her teenage skunk before he went out to drive.

Answer: She hollered out, "don't stink and drive".

Joke: What did the mother Firefly say to her daughter Firefly when she was going away? She said;

Answer: "You glow girl"

Why did the football coach go to the phone booth?

To get his Quarter-Back!

Chapter 7 - Nationality Jokes

Joke: So, one day a German man and a Jewish man had a small discussion. So, the Jewish man asked the German man a question; "Why do you Jews answer a question with a question?" And the German man replied; "Why shouldn't we?"

Joke: A week later the same men were discussing small talk at this time. Now the German man asked the Jewish man, "I wonder if infants have as much fun in infancy, as adults do in adultery?"

Joke: What nationality are you when you're in the washroom or bathroom?

Answer: Your, European.

What did the Atlantic Ocean say to the Pacific Ocean when the departed?

They didn't say anything.
They just waved!

Chapter 8 - Clown Jokes

Joke: What did one cannibal say to the other cannibal when he was eating the clown?

Answer: He said; "Mmmmmm.... something taste funny."

...

Joke: Why don't alligators eat clowns?

Answer: They taste funny (m.a)

Joke: Two Clowns were upset with each other at the circus and the one clowns told the other, 'I have a bone to pick with you'.

Surprised the other clown asked, 'What kind of bone'. He responded, 'A funny Bone' (m.a)

...

Joke: What happened when the Clown ate spoiled meat?

Answer: He felt funny (m.a)

...

Joke: What do you call kid clowns running in circles?
Answer: Clowning Around (m.a)

What is the best way to clean a telephone?

With Dial soap!

Chapter 9 - State Jokes

Joke: What is a dentist a favorite suburb in Illinois?

Answer: Flossmoor, Illinois.

...

Joke: What did the Atlantic Ocean say to the Pacific Ocean when they departed?

Answer: They didn't say anything. They just waved.

Joke: Out of all the 50 states which one has the best vision?

Answer: The state of Mississippi. It has four 'eyes'. E-Y-E-S.

...

Joke: How of all the 50 states, which one appears the most sickest out of all of them?

Answer: Illinois. Ill-inois.

...

Joke: How do people in Hawaii laugh quietly?

Answer: They laugh with a-low-'ha'

Joke: In the state of Alaska, how do the natives and Eskimos build their houses?

Answer: They use Ig-loo.

...

Joke: If all the cars in the world were pink, what would we have?

Answer: A pink-car-nation.

...

Joke: How did children learn to read the clock in New York City?

Answer: They learn by going to Times Square

Joke: How can you tell when Will Smith has been walking in the snow in Chicago?

Answer: You just look for fresh prints.

...

Joke: The redbrick was on one corner of the block and the green brick was on one other corner of the block. Where was the White House located?

Answer: Washington D.C.

Why did the little boy Toby throw his CD's into the fire?

Because he wanted to burn some CD's

Chapter 10 - Music Jokes

Joke: How is a piano like a slippery sidewalk in Chicago?

Answer: If you don't 'C-Sharp', you will 'B flat'.

...

What do you call a drummer that loses his drumsticks?

Answer: You call him a 'band' conductor.

Joke: What kind of music do they play in a soda factory?

Answer: They play 'Pop' music

Why did the little boy throw pennies at his little sister's head?

Because he tried to knock some 'cents' into her.

Chapter 11 - Funny / Corny Jokes

Joke: Why did the little boy Toby throw his CDs into the fire?

Answer: Because he wanted to burn some CD's

...

Joke: If March winds bring April showers. What do Mayflowers bring?

Answer: The pilgrims

Joke: What kind of waves can't you ride?

Answer: You can't ride micro-waves

...

True Story: Traveling back from Sacramento, California, I was on Southwest Airlines and I asked the flight attendant did she have any more souvenir plastic **WINGS**?

Mind you, it was dark outside. And I began to sing the song; 'I believe I can fly, I believe I can touch the sky, I dream about it every night and day, spread my **WINGS** and fly away. I believe I can fly'.

Joke: Why did the little boy throw pennies at his little sister's head?

Answer: Because he tried to knock some 'cents' into her.

...

Joke: What is the best way to clean a telephone?

Answer: With a dial soap.

...

Joke: Why was the man afraid to sit in his chair?

Answer: Because it was armed.

Joke: Why is it so hard to play tennis in the library?

Answer: Because of all the racket.

...

Joke: What did one finger say to the other finger on Valentine's Day?

Answer: Thumb-body loves you

Joke: Why did the lady walk around with cosmetics in her hair?

Answer: Because she couldn't 'make-up' her mind.

True Story: It was a sunny day in town and I had a talk with my mailman. I said to him in a very humorous voice, "I'm so glad I'm a male-man". He could not stop laughing and he smiled and grinned the rest of the day. A male, M-A-L-E man

...

Joke: Why was the groom mad on his wedding day?

Answer: Because the bride married the Best-man

...

Joke: What is the best way to find your way in a very, very dark castle?

Answer: You just turn on the 'Knight-light'

Joke: What starts with the letter E, and ends with the letter E?

Answer: Envelope

Joke: When is a door not a door?

Answer: When it's a-jar.

...

Joke: Why isn't your nose 12 inches long?

Answer: Because then it would be a foot.

...

Joke: What do you say to God when he sneezes?

Answer:_____

Joke: What did the hat tell the tie before they departed?

Answer: You go ahead and I will hang around.

...

Joke: What are the strongest days of the week?

Answer: Monday through Friday. The rest our 'weak' ends

Joke: One day a man went on a fishing trip in a remote island and unfortunately, he got shipwrecked. Three days later, a little bottle came up on the shore and he was so very, very happy.

The man took the little bottle and rubbed it and suddenly a big giant genie appeared. And he replied, "Mr... You have three wishes". So, the man thought to himself OK.

Number one; "I wish for a brand-new Cadillac". *briiiing* A Cadillac appeared with all the options and amenities and the man was very, very happy.

And the genie replied, "You have a second wish". He said, "I wish that I was a millionaire and I won a million dollars". So, he took the million dollars and put it in the trunk of the Cadillac and as he was driving on the island, he turned on his radio and the station was playing a commercial, [singing] "ohhh I wish I was an Oscar Meyer wiener... That is all I want to really be." So, he turned into a wiener unfortunately.

...

Joke: What did cloud number one, say to one cloud number two.

Answer: He replied two's are plenty and three's a cloud.

Joke: What do you call President Washington's false teeth?

Answer: You call them 'Presi-dentures'.

...

Joke: What do lawyers say, right before they go to bed at night?

Answer: They say, "I rest my case"

...

Joke: What did one casket asked the other casket?

Answer: Is that you coughing?

Joke: What do you call someone that wears black and goes around and around?

Answer: A witch that is stuck in a revolving door

...

Joke: Why must a bicycle stand on a bicycle stand?

Answer: Because it's 'two-tired'

...

Joke: What do you call a rifle that has given birth to her little child?

Answer: Call it a son-of-a-gun.

Joke: What are the three rings of marriage?

Answer: The first ring of marriage is an engagement ring.

The second ring of marriage is a wedding ring.

The third ring of marriage is 'Suffer-ring'.

...

Joke: Why is it so hard for G-Unit to get on the bus?

Answer: Because he only had 50 cents

Joke: Why did Tiger Woods wear two pairs of pants to the golf Open?

Answer: In case he had a 'hole-in-one'.

...

Joke: Why didn't the bowling professionals go to the bowling game?

Answer: Because they were on 'strike'

...

Joke: Why did Cinderella go home with the photographer?

Answer: Because her 'prints' had not come in yet.

Joke: If you threw a blue stone into the Red Sea what would you have?

Answer: A 'wetstone'

...

Joke: Why did the football coach go to the phone booth?

Answer: To get his 'quarter' back.

...

Joke: Where do TV's go when they want a vacation?

Answer: They go to a very remote island.

Joke: How much do pirates pay to get their ears pierced?

Answer: They pay a 'buck-an-ear', a buc-can-neer. Buccaneer. OK.

...

Joke: What happened to the picture that was on the wall?

Answer: He got 'framed'.

Why did the children eat their homework?

Because the teacher told them that is was a piece of cake

Chapter 12 - School Jokes

Joke: What do you do with a nuclear physicist when he dies?

Answer: You bury him. Spelled capital B-A-R-I-U-M.

...

Joke: If two is a plenty, and three's a crowd. What is four and five?

Answer: Nine. Duh!

Joke: Why did the children eat their homework?

Answer: Because the teacher told them that it was a piece of cake.

...

Joke: What happened to the plant that was in the window seal in the math class?

Answer: It begin to grow its square root

What did the tree say to the math teacher when he passed by?

He said, 'Gee-I'm-a-tree, you get it Geometry!

Joke: Why didn't the boy do his history homework?

Answer: Because he said to himself, 'Let bygones be bygones'

...

Joke: what do books take with them when they leave the library?

Answer: They take pagers.

Why did the little boy wear his T-shirt to school wet?

Because the T-shirt said on the back label:
'Wash and Wear'

Chapter 13 - Police Jokes

Joke: For what do you call a policeman that works in the bed all day?

Answer: You call them; Under-cover-cop.

...

Joke: Did you hear about the head floating in Lake Michigan, two and a half weeks ago? A Chicago policeman walks by the floating head and the head tells the Chicago policeman I ain't got nooooooo body. Get it?

What do you call a policeman that works in the bed all day?

You call them an Under-cover Cop!

Thank You for Laughing with me.

THE END

visit my site for more Jokes

www.BJtheJokeMan.com

Made in the USA
Lexington, KY
31 December 2017